OXFORD
IN OLD PHOTOGRAPHS

HIGH STREET, OXFORD.

Oxford agrees with me splendidly, the people here vie one with the other in giving one a real good time.

OXFORD
IN OLD PHOTOGRAPHS

COLLECTED BY
JUDI CATON

Budding
BOOKS

A Budding Book

First published in 1988 by Alan Sutton Publishing Limited

This edition published in 1998 by Budding Books,
an imprint of Sutton Publishing Limited
Phoenix Mill · Thrupp · Stroud · Gloucestershire GL5 2BU

A catalogue record for this book is available from the British Library

ISBN 1-84015-072-6

Typesetting and origination by
Sutton Publishing Limited.
Printed in Great Britain by
WBC Limited, Bridgend, Mid-Glamorgan.

CONTENTS

A birdseye view of central Oxford, taken from Magdalen Tower before the building of the Examination Schools in 1882.

INTRODUCTION

The City of Oxford conjures up images of 'Dreaming Spires', of May balls and May mornings, of scouts and bedels and of examinations and eternal youth. But there is, and always has been, another Oxford – the one in which people live all their lives, not just their undergraduate years. It is not entirely separate from the first, for Town and Gown have to a large extent together developed its traditions and customs, into the shared pastimes and activities of today. A visitor to the City might easily be able to distinguish the different groups of people celebrating May morning on Magdalen Bridge, but he would undoubtedly recognise that people from all parts of Oxford come to mark the festival.

The other Oxford has strong images of its own. Lines of Bullnose Morrises and Minis, and workers streaming from factory gates on bicycles heading for nearby housing estates, spring readily to mind. But William Morris became Lord Nuffield and endowed Nuffield College. Oxford's history and development and that of its people has, since the establishment of the University, been a subtle entwining of University and Town traditions. This book concentrates on the latter, not in order to highlight the inevitable contrasts but because each deserves its own special treatment.

The photographic record of the City is dominated, as Oxford has always been, by the Rivers Thames and Cherwell. Like so many of the settlements in the Upper

Thames Valley, Oxford lies on a gravel spur where the main river, the Thames, is joined by a tributary, the Cherwell. The rivers and their floodplains have over the centuries both defined and confined the settlement. In the Middle Ages, for instance, Oxford was renowned as an easily defendable inland site defined by its rivers, an important attribute in its history. Today, the necessity for bridges confines Oxford's road system. The rivers are now a constraining factor in solving Oxford's traffic problems.

If the rivers have defined and confined the settlement, they have also given to Oxford a great deal of its character. The trade and industry, communications, floods and frustration, rowing races, beautiful scenes, and the sheer fun, all given to Oxford by the rivers and more recently the canal, leap out of these pages.

The value of Oxford's position, however, at the confluences of these two rivers in the very centre of England was not recognised until the Anglo-Saxon period for the evidence for early settlement in Oxford is fairly slight. Some Neolithic material has been found in the area of Christ Church. Bronze Age burial mounds can be seen on air photographs of Port Meadow, and there is a linear group of barrows in the University Parks. A Beaker burial too was found in excavations at The Hamel in St Thomas's Street.

The Romans regarded the Oxford area as an industrial zone, where abundant local clay led to the establishment of one of the five major production centres of Roman-British pottery. Industry, therefore, has a very long tradition in Oxford. In the Roman period the area produced vast quantities of a wide range of domestic vessels including mixing bowls, and more elegant painted table wares.

The Romans, though, did not build a town. They crossed the floodplain to the north and south of the present city with roads. The southern one probably served the potteries, and acted as a link to the main Dorchester to Alcester road.

This main Roman road was eventually replaced by a north-south road running through Oxford on the line of St Aldates and the Abingdon Road. A crossing over the river may have existed here by the late eighth century during the reign of King Offa of Mercia. It was very important in the development of Oxford as a town, for the Thames was the boundary between the Kingdoms of Mercia to the north and Wessex to the south. Oxford would have been a frontier town of considerable strategic importance. Certainly by the ninth or tenth century, a stone ford, the Oxen Ford, from which the town took its name, crossed the floodplain at this point.

If the evidence for the Oxen Ford is combined with that for the foundation of a monastery by St Frideswide (c.727) then Oxford almost certainly became a town in the late Saxon period. The foundation of a monastery is generally supposed to have led to a lay settlement which grew into a town. In any event by the early tenth century Oxford was a defended *burh*, listed in the *Burghal Hideage*, under the jurisdiction of Alfred, King of the West Saxons.

Alfred's son Edward the Elder took control of the town in 911, and it was probably he who planned Oxford's streets and defences. Its tradition as a pottery producing area was re-established in the tenth century too. The bulk of all the coarse pottery used in London at this time travelled down the Thames from Oxford. The town's natural attributes were again contributing to its prosperity.

The Normans almost immediately recognised Oxford's strategic advantages. Robert D'Oilly built the Castle, of which only the motte now remains, in 1071, completely re-jigging the western streets and defences of the town. He also rebuilt in stone the Grandpont, now Folly Bridge, one of the biggest Norman constructions in Britain.

With all this major engineering under way it is a surprise to find that the Domesday Book recorded Oxford as a poor and wasted place in 1086. It apparently had very many derelict properties. Some think the town had not recovered from being burnt in 1009 following the massacre of the Danes, others that the building of the Castle and the Conquest itself caused upheaval. Whatever the reasons Oxford soon recovered, probably as a result of its geographic advantages now enhanced by Robert D'Oilly's causeway.

In the twelfth century Oxford was the meeting place of great national assemblies. Here the English and the Danes agreed to observe King Edgar's law, and the English barons swore allegiance to Henry II. Not far north at Woodstock English kings frequently held court. Oxford became one of England's foremost towns. It was centrally placed, at the convergence of many important roads, protected by a castle, walls and rivers, containing markets, trades and industries, and attracting those monastic foundations which were to make it into a place of learning. By the 1260s when Merton, the first true college was founded, Oxford had seen thousands of years of settlement, over one thousand years of industry, and at least three hundred and fifty years as a town. The growth of the University cemented and increased Oxford's importance and the city was a prosperous place throughout the Middle Ages.

The next major upheaval came when Oxford's defendability and central position made it attractive as a choice for the headquarters of the royalist army after the battle of Edgehill in 1642. New defences were planned, and some of them were built. Buildings were requisitioned, and King and Court moved in. From then until Charles I's surrender after the last siege of Oxford in June 1646, Oxford was the royalist capital of England.

From the seventeenth century until the earliest photographs in this book, from the 1860s, the most radical alterations made to Oxford were probably the building of the Victorian suburbs and public buildings. Some of these, and their later demise are captured in these pages. The comparatively recent and very recent wholesale demolition of medieval and later houses in central Oxford, and their replacement with new shopping precincts, public buildings and modern housing has probably had the biggest impact on the city since the Normans' building schemes.

JUDI CATON
March 1988

KISSING IN OXFORDSHIRE
[By One Who's Had Some.]

A Good-Looking Young Fellow has lately been "doing" this County, and has made notes with reference to KISSING in different parts.

HE found that the **THAME** Girls keep quite still until well kissed, and then say "I think you ought to be ashamed of yourself."

An **ABINGDON** Girl when kissed closes her eyes in ecstacy, and murmurs: "Do it again, George."

An **OXFORD** Girlie says "Oh!" very softly, and suggests a stroll to

WILLOW WALK.

A Marriageable Maiden of **WALLINGFORD** on being kissed tries to look stern, fails, then slides her little hand into that of the bold, bad man, and in a voice as soft as butter, whispers tenderly, "Won't Mother be pleased!"

Whilst the Girls of **BANBURY** say: "Well, I never thought it of you, and I am very much surprised, and I hope you won't try to do it again; but don't let us stop here where it is light, let us go out of the town where no one will see us."

[REG.]

Good Old Oxford

From one merry ole Sole to another.

Titchfield Series, Copyright

No. 301.

10

Carfax or Four Ways at the very centre of Oxford. This view is looking from St Aldates to St Martin's Church which was demolished in 1896.

Only a few years later St Martin's has gone and Carfax looks far more familiar. Could the stall be a forerunner of the Kebab vans?

Another view of Carfax taken 80 years ago. Even then a policeman stood guard and pedestrians thronged the streets. At least they knew where the trams went; buses are less predictable.

Looking up the High Street from Longwall Street on the right, to Queens College. In 1897 when this photograph was taken, trams and horse-drawn vehicles filled the streets.

This fierce looking group were in fact 'Beating the Bounds' in Longwall Street in 1907.

Still one of Oxford's most beautiful streets, this is Merton Street in about 1900. Grove Street, now Magpie Lane, is on the left.

Two portraits of Alfred Street between the Bear Inn and the High Street. The top photograph was taken in 1913, the bottom one in 1962.

Two small boys stand in Blue Boar Street in 1901. Despite the sunny day the town street looks pot-holed and muddy.

Two different boys pose at the other end of the street. The old Public Library became the Museum of Oxford in 1976.

St Aldates nearly 90 years ago. The eye was drawn towards Tom Tower and Christ Church just as it is today, despite the tempting, and to our eyes exotic, Oyster Bar.

By 1930 the tempting oyster bar has become a furrier's, and Morris cars dominate St Aldates.

This stretch of Oxford's medieval wall runs between the site of the South Gate in St Aldates, and that of the Littlegate in St Ebbes Street. It may not be deliberately visited like the stretch in New College, but it is well frequented, forming one side of Brewer Street.

Street cleaners pause for a break as they prepare to tidy up Carfax. The town looks empty but it must be early morning as the milk pram at the top of Queen Street shows.

Looking up Queen Street to the Church of All Saints.

Queen Street looking towards New Road, all decorated in celebration of the Diamond Jubilee of Queen Victoria in 1897.

The motte of Oxford Castle built by Robert D'Oilly in 1071. This view was taken in the 1940s when it was still accessible to the public and covered in trees.

In the 1970s, All Saints church is undergoing conversion to become Lincoln College Library, and Queen Street has been paved.

A fascinating view of Cornmarket in the 1920s. The Saxon Tower of the Church of St Michael at the Northgate still marks the edge of the old city, but none of the shops are recognisable.

Cornmarket looking north from Market Street in 1907. The blue pipes of the Clarendon Centre have not replaced the old Clarendon Hotel.

Traffic and queues are an all too common sight in Cornmarket, but this was taken in the 1950s!

Cornmarket Street looking from St Michael's Street, to George Street and Magdalen Street. The Plough Inn at the bottom left is now Austin Reed the fashion shop.

The courtyard of the Golden Cross Hotel seen above in 1907, and below in 1970. This famous coaching inn, formerly called the Angel, has now been converted into a shopping precinct which links Cornmarket with the Covered Market.

George Street in 1911. The street was outside the medieval city but is very much part of the centre of Oxford today. Nos 41–53 Bulwarks Lane and the City of Oxford High School for Boys can be seen on the right.

Bone floors were a common construction in Oxfordshire. This one, made from the ends of cattle and horse metapodials, was photographed during demolition in George Street in September 1894.

These old houses in George Street were demolished to make way for the City of Oxford High School for Boys built in 1878.

Above ground demolition this time. The house was in Victoria Place off George Street.

Still in George Street, this was a classroom erected in the Second World War.

A birdseye view of Gloucester Green Bus Station in 1939. The City of Oxford Boys School which was used as the Ticket Office for many years has been retained in the recent development scheme.

Without the photograph below it is difficult to place the bottom of George Street in the 1920s. Not only have many buildings been demolished or rebuilt, but the provisions made for the motor car now dominate the scene.

The corner of Cornmarket Street, Magdalen Street and Broad Street in July 1914. The Oxford Drug Company is still trading there, but the whole corner is now taken up by Dillons bookshop.

Blackwell's on the other hand have been trading in Oxford's Broad Street for a long time. This view with the magnificent horse-drawn cab waiting outside is Edwardian, but Benjamin Henry Blackwell opened his shop at Number 50 Broad Street in 1879.

Broad Street lives up to its name, forming the perfect scene for this procession of school children celebrating Queen Victoria's Jubilee on 6 June 1887. Why does it always rain on such occasions?

The shops in Magdalen Street have changed considerably in seventy years. Taphouses saw Elliston and Cavell come and go but finally moved to the High Street when the Debenham empire filled this part of the street.

Since 1880 the rails have gone from the steps of Oxford's famous Martyrs Memorial. The taxis, though, are still there, if somewhat changed.

One of Oxford's most elegant streets, Beaumont Street. This view shows off its Georgian houses looking towards the Oxford Playhouse on the right, and the Institute of Archaeology on the left.

The Ashmolean Museum seen here from the Stables Entrance of the Randolph Hotel.

On the King's birthday, 23 June 1936, disaster struck at No 27 St Clements. The crowd stand across the street watching the efforts of the firemen.

Albion Place off St Clements was demolished in the 1930s. The Victorian houses backed on to a small courtyard where the residents used the shared stand pipe for their water supply.

The back of No. 15 Caroline Street which was demolished in 1935. How dark these houses must have been – the windows were minute.

It was not all destruction in St Clements in the 1930s. The construction of these houses in Morrell Avenue was well under way.

A birdseye view of Divinity Road in 1895. It must have been taken from St Mary and St John's Church and it looks towards the Oxford Workhouse behind the street.

Taking tea in a Divinity Road garden in about 1900. Perhaps such elegant scenes take place today, though no doubt without the elaborate headgear.

Rebuilding a wall at Nazareth House, Cowley Road, in the 1920s.

Joseph Cotterell's butchers and grocers shop on the Cowley Road, c.1905.

Cowley Road during the First World War looks almost like a country lane. St Mary and St John's Church is in the background.

Partial flooding in Cowley Road in 1902. Travelling was very hard work for horses and pedestrians alike.

The Lees and Johnsons were the two biggest families in Cowley. Nearly everyone was related to one or other or both. This is a mixed group of Lees and Johnsons c. 1908.

Mr Dick King on the left had a workshop in Hockmore Street behind the old Nelson pub. The photograph was taken before 1900 and Mr Kearsey the owner of the newly-completed cart stands on the right.

The Stocks Tree in Cowley before 1907 when the tree was cut down. The barn of White's farm is on the right.

A delightful view of Cowley Parish Church before its restoration in 1864.

A smiling group of children pictured at a 'Juvenile Tea' of the Cowley Court of the Ancient Order of Foresters. In those days (1930s) this friendly society had 2–300 members in Cowley. Every Friday 'sick pay' was distributed to members off work.

This rural scene took place as recently as 1974 when Snowdrop cottage was rethatched.

Morris Motors works in the Garsington Road in the 1930s.

Cowley's most famous son motoring with his wife and Mr and Mrs Harry Burrows on the Garsington Road in 1911. Two years later W.R. Morris produced his own first car.

Mr R. Gibbons, landlord of the Cricketer's Arms, Temple Road, with a pony trap full of children. The photograph was taken at the junction of Hollow Way and Horspath Road c. 1898.

Temple Cowley from Southfield Golf Course, showing Crescent Road c. 1900.

A close up of Crescent Road, Cowley, from a postcard sent in 1906. Whoever sent the card wrote 'This is Cowley on mud, all roads are like this one'.

At the beginning of the First World War, Sandhill and Jacob's Pit are viewed from the stooks of hay on Lye Hill.

Henry Taunt's famous and irresistible study of children playing ducks and drakes in the sheep washing place along Barracks Lane, Cowley. In the background some golfers make their way to the Southfield Golf Course. This delightful scene was captured at the inauspicious time of July 1914.

Temple Cowley school photograph. The class of 1900.

Temple Cowley girls' school with Mrs N. Parker sitting on the extreme left of the front row. In 1911 pinafores and lace-up black boots were *de rigueur.*

Cowley in the 1950s. The rear view of a house in Marshall Road, just the other side of Hollow Way from the semi-rural scenes of Temple Cowley.

The occupants of the house in the previous picture pose for the camera.

Parents and children of Blackbird Leys in 1958. They look very happy but in fact they are protesting. Mrs Green and Mrs Bromley are walking their children Valerie, Pauline, Paul, Marian and Nigel one and a half miles to school at Rose Hill because the Cowley Airfield School was full. They moved in before any facilities were available.

Boys will always find somewhere to lark about. These children were photographed playing in Blackbird Leys in 1971.

The 'Cutteslowe Walls Affair' is a famous piece of Oxford history. People from the Cutteslowe Council estate came out on 13 May 1935, to demonstrate angrily against the developer who had erected a wall between Wolsey and Carlton Roads to separate them from his private dwellings.

Not until March 1959 was the wall demolished. A group of Oxford City Councillors watch the workmen knocking out the bricks. From left to right they are: Mrs Williams, Alderman Lower, Alderman Mrs Lower, Councillor Mrs Gibbs and Councillor E Gibbs.

Presumably this was set up for the camera, but the children's march through the gap left by the demolition of the walls admirably signifies the final joining of two Cutteslowe communities.

The gentleman in the top hat was standing on the last weir bridge, with Iffley Manor behind him, in 1885. Is he playing poohsticks, or just watching the ducks?

The Norman splendour of Iffley Church taken from the opposite bank of the river, framed by the trees.

The toll keeper with his companion at Iffley Lock.

Iffley has a more well-known popular tradition – the celebration of May Day. These children were carrying the traditional garlands in 1953.

Floyds Row from St Aldates in 1910. The name is all that remains of this charming street today, between the Music Faculty and the Police Station.

Twenty-two years later one side of Floyds Row has already gone and the rest of the now rather sad-looking houses were demolished in 1935. The new showroom of Morris Motors, now Oxford Crown Court, can be seen on the right.

This delightful part of Oxford is also the site of one of the major pieces of Norman engineering in Britain. Robert D'Oilly built Grandpont ('The Great Bridge') now called Folly Bridge, though only three arches of his bridge, still accessible by punt, survive. Salter brothers still offer pleasure trips and boats for hire in the summer months.

Another view of Folly Bridge taken in 1876. The base of the crane beside the bridge can still be seen but the building which was part of Salter's business is now the thriving pub, The Head of the River.

Robert D'Oilly's arches under repair. In 1981 a watermain burst on Folly Bridge damaging the wall and all traffic was stopped for a time. Major repairs were needed before two-way traffic could be restored.

In this part of Oxford there is water everywhere and a backwater flows right under Grandpont House. This view was taken from the towing path in around 1900.

The Island and Folly Bridge from the west in 1904. The crenellated roof of Folly House can just be seen on the right. Summer punting is just as popular today but not so many people wear boaters.

The other residents of the river beside Folly Bridge, the swans, are seen here in large numbers. Twenty-five years ago the old houses on the other side of the river on Friars Wharf were still inhabited.

After many years of negotiation, the houses on Friars Wharf were finally put back. The swans are once again fed on both sides of the river.

The Great Western Railway lies behind the houses of Grandpont and the Abingdon Road. Floods, like this one in November 1894, could be quite a problem.

The problem could be even worse on the roads. In January 1915 the low-lying meadows flooded and the water washed right over the Abingdon Road. Aldens the butchers had already moved into Eastwyke Farm on the right, and to the left is the site of the road to be aptly known as Lake Street.

Floods could be fun too! Mr A. Jefferies the Oxford City goalkeeper paddles a friend up the Abingdon Road on 17 March 1947.

New bridges make a big difference to the life of a town surrounded by water. Donnington Road Bridge was not constructed until 1961. While the motor cars awaited a new freedom, the life of the swans and rowers continued as normal.

An example of barge power. Floating a section of the Gasworks Bridge into position over 100 years ago.

Mrs Elizabeth Cotmore who ran a market garden on Boars Hill with her husband Charles, seen here in 1900. She drove a covered wagon round Oxford to supply goods to market stall-holders.

It is difficult not to worry that the diligent workman re-laying cobbles is in some danger from trams. One hundred years before Don Millers, Selfridges and Bonn Square the junction between Castle Street and New Road was a busy part of Oxford.

As little as twenty years ago, the same junction looks just as unfamiliar. It emphasises how much the recent Westgate development has altered Oxford's old street layouts.

In Castle Street at the turn of the century. The Queen's Head and the Salvation Army citadel are on the right.

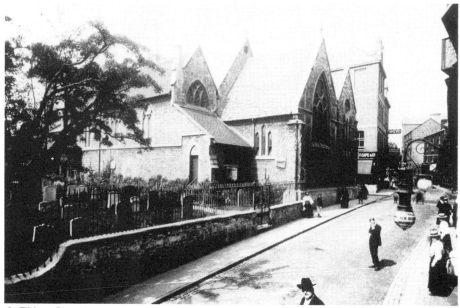

St Ebbes Church and churchyard stood out clearly in 1907. Now the church is surrounded by one of Oxford's busiest shopping areas.

Boys contemplate their hoops in the heart of Oxford's old St Ebbes. This is Church Street in 1907, one of the streets which has completely disappeared under the Westgate Centre.

Thick rope washing lines crossed Godfrey's Yard in St Ebbes on a summer day in 1914.

This house in Albert Place, off Castle Street, at the beginning of the First World War. Without modern appliances washing was always hanging out to dry.

Broken windows and rubbish offer another view of the old St Ebbes. This family were photographed in Chaundy's yard in June 1914.

Twenty-five years ago, soon before it was pulled down, Blackfriars Road, St Ebbes was a rather overgrown place.

To local residents St Ebbes was home. Mr and Mrs J. Hedges of 36 Albert Street looked stunned and resigned as they watched the demolition on 11 August 1967.

Mrs Rogers at the door of the family business, the Bijou Stores in St Ebbes, in the 1920s. Her husband started the business and concentrated on the musical side. Her son Stan became a well-known Oxford band leader.

Cambridge Terrace leading to Clarks Row, St Ebbes just over twenty years ago.

Long before Blackwell's and the Oxford Fire Service came to Rewley Road, two pubs and the Railway Hotel were doing business. This view looks towards Park End Street and Hollybush Row.

A donkey cart is the centre of attention in Hollybush Row, in the part of Oxford called St Thomas's in 1907.

Canal and river side by side in Upper Fisher Row. Punts are stationed on the river, a barge on the canal. Hythe Bridge crosses them both.

Looking from Hythe Bridge down Upper Fisher Row to the remains of Rewley Abbey on the left. The boundary wall of Worcester College skirts the canal on the right.

Some of the 'essential Oxford' can be seen in this view taken in 1954. The spire of Nuffield College towers above the Norman castle mound and the boys guiding the horse and pleasure boat along the canal in Lower Fisher Row.

The famous view of Middle Fisher Row taken by Henry Taunt c.1885. It is remarkable not just for the quality of the photograph but for the charm of the seventeenth-century houses, and for the beauty of the cobbled waterfront.

Forty years after Taunt's study the seventeenth-century houses look run down and Pacey's Bridge needs attention.

By 1954 Pacey's Bridge has been completely renewed, but the houses are in sad need of renovation. They were eventually all demolished.

Riverside life on Middle Fisher Row in the 1920s. The children stand beneath Pacey's Bridge.

The same waterfront, but a close-up of Abel Beesley punting a load of rushes upstream to the Beesley Rushworks at the end of Upper Fisher Row.

Beesley's Rushworks. The Osier stands on the right with some completed eel traps.

The Botley Road railway bridge in 1904. The old Gate House pub is still in business. Miss Ada Podson's Temperance Hotel is on the right.

A carriage moves towards Oseney Bridge seen from the Temperance Hotel in 1919.

Advertising boards covered the front of the London Midland and Scottish Railway station in the 1930s. The building is now a garage.

The entrance to Oxford's Great Western Railway Station in the 1930s. If only all tickets for trains after 8.30 a.m. were still cheap today. No doubt the journey took longer and commuters were few and far between.

The crowds all stand at the water's edge in front of the Railway Station in 1875. Some punt across, some go by horse-drawn carriage.

In 1970 the old station of the Great Western Railway was still the town's Railway Station.

Oseney from Oseney Bridge in 1974. The area to the far left of the river is the site of the great medieval monastery of the Augustinian Canons, Oseney Abbey. Only fragments survive under a modern cemetery, the railway and Oseney Industrial Estate. To the right, East Street on Oseney Island is threatened by the swelling river.

Over 100 years ago Oseney's stone bridge collapsed and had to be replaced by a new metal one.

A recent view of Oseney's typical housing. This is Bridge Street in the cold winter of 1982.

Floods have always been more of a problem in Oxford than snow. On 21 June 1903 the Thames overflowed filling Bridge Street.

People were forced to take to punts as a close-up of the Bridge Street floods shows. The inhabitants of Oseney seem most intrigued by the presence of a photographer!

Arguments still rage about whether to by-pass the Botley Road. In 1949 drivers were stopped to answer questions. The cinema, first converted by MFI and now demolished, can be seen on the right.

In 1924 it was thought that the answer to the Botley Road's traffic problems was to widen it. The workmen are just in front of Seacourt Bridge.

The mayor's party punting across the river at New Hinksey in 1892.

The delightful hamlet of Binsey is accessible by road from the Botley Road or on foot from Port Meadow. Its pub, the Perch, is a favourite haunt of Oxford people, especially on a Sunday. However, Binsey's great attractions are that it is a country place only a slight walk from the city, and it has the famous St Margaret's Well which is rich in legend and folk tale. This view of the Binsey houses dates from the 1950s.

Binsey tow path in winter. This is one of Henry Taunt's irresistible studies of Oxford over 100 years ago. You can feel the cold.

Some of Jericho has been demolished in recent years. This part of Nelson Street came down in 1976.

Barney's demolition contractors did the work in Nelson Street. This is tea break for the men – at the table too!

Eighty years ago a ferry took passengers from the end of Combe Road across the canal to the footpath. The ferryman and his family pose for the camera.

A boatman with his horse and three children beside the canal in around 1900. The little girl wears the typical head-dress of the canal people.

Frank Restall's Building Supplies at Hayfield Wharf nearly 100 years ago. The women on the barges are wearing typical head-dress and clothing.

Miss Jean Humphries with the barrow, and Mrs Rose Skinner shovelling at the Juxon Street wharf in Jericho. The two ladies were employed to unload coal barges in 1956.

Almost as much fun as the seaside! Children returning home to Cardigan Street from school when Jericho was flooded on 8 June 1955.

A recent view of Canal Street, Jericho, with the tower of St Barnabas Church.

Another recent view showing the new housing built on the Hinkins and Frewin site at the bottom of Canal Street. St Barnabas Church still dominates the Jericho landscape, but the barges, once used to transport goods are now pleasure boats.

Bossom's boatyard on the left and Beesley's on the right at Medley next to Port Meadow in around 1895.

A frosty day on the towing path at Medley and Rainbow Bridge 100 years ago.

When Port Meadow floods or freezes it becomes a natural playground for the people of Oxford. In June 1904 people came out to sail or watch the boating.

The Banbury Road at the North Oxford suburb, Summertown, in May 1929. The houses are Nos. 230–240.

Summerhill House in Summertown was built in 1823. It was owned by James Ryman who is posing on the steps.

This young lady provides a central focus for Taunt's study of the River Cherwell above Marston Ferry in 1885.

A stretch of the river in the University Parks. Waterlilies, rushes and bushes make the going difficult for boats.

The River Cherwell frozen near the Victoria Arms at Marston in around 1887. This pub is a very popular lunch stop for parties punting along the Cherwell. It has recently been re-developed and the buildings now take up all of the enclosure.

The small street beside the paper mill at Wolvercote is naturally called Mill Road. On the right are some residents of the 1900s.

The Nun's Chapel ruins, part of Godstow Nunnery across the frozen river in 1895.

In late summer the flow of water under Wolvercote Bridge leaves room for a young man on a cycle.

Looking east down Godstow Road, Wolvercote, at the turn of the century.

The splendid view of 'Dreaming Spires' from Headington Hill House, once the home of the Morrell family and now that of Robert Maxwell and his family.

Hundreds of children watching the entertainment at a Headington Hill Hall garden party. The hat was clearly a compulsory item at least for such an occasion.

Butter-making outside the dairy at Headington Hill Hall during the First World War. The gentleman stands beside a churn while the white-capped lady prepares the butter worker.

Students at the Domestic Training School for Young Girls in their class photograph in 1913. The school was started by Mrs G. H. Morrell to help orphans and other disadvantaged young girls. Those who are not wearing caps have their hair parted severely in the middle.

A Headington street in the 1930s. Headington has its own old centre but this part of Oxford must have been a bright new suburb when the photograph was taken.

In contrast this view shows Horwood's Pit beneath number 24 Beaumont Road in Headington Quarry. Stone quarrying began here soon after 1400 and was an important source of material for Oxford buildings, as well as a traditional trade and way of life for local people.

The attractive footbridge across Headington Hill Road in the depths of the winter of 1979. The road is way down below on the left.

Barton Village road, now just north of the Oxford ring road, was a peaceful place in 1947.

The Fox Inn in Barton Lane, Headington was demolished between 1935 and 1940 and rebuilt on the by-pass. This photograph was taken in 1898.

The exodus from the plant of the Pressed Steel Company at Cowley in 1950. The company began as the result of an agreement between William Morris and Edward E. Budd and went through several permutations. In 1930 Morris Motors sold all their shares in the company which became Pressed Steel Fisher. Since the war it merged with Morris Motors in the British Motor Corporation, and then became British Leyland, now Leyland Cars.

Morris Garages Limited in Holywell Street. Here, Morris, who is seated in the car on the right, opened his cycle business, transformed by 1912 into a car works.

Morris Motors Limited car export line in 1941.

Morris Garages Limited, St Aldates showrooms at night. This building is now Oxford Crown Court, but how spectacular it looked in 1932 doing the job it was meant for, drawing the eye to the cars.

Not everyone at Morris Motors made cars. These ladies were the firm's telephone exchange operators in 1936.

Not all of Morris's businesses were to do with cars. This is the treadmill of the Nuffield Press conveyor belt in 1929.

Pressers on the factory floor at Osberton Radiators in 1930.

The sales representatives of Allens of Cowley lined up in their Bullnose Morrises. The company was founded in 1868. John Allen was an early manager who bought the business for £13,000 in 1897. Now the company called Grove Allen is American-owned.

Tuckwells used a Bullnose Morris in the 1920s to pull their wagon from the goods shed of the London Midland and Scottish Railway.

Behind the scenes at Coopers Oxford Marmalade Factory in Park End Street in 1910. The employees manage to make marmalade-making seem a somewhat leisurely if very orderly affair. The building now houses the Oxford Antiques Centre.

One of Oxford's breweries, Morrell's, is still in St Thomas's Street, though this picture was taken around 1900.

Some deliveries in Oxford have to be made by river. These barrels in July 1972 were destined for the Isis Tavern on the way to Iffley.

The owner and his employees gather outside the St Giles Brickworks in the 1880s. The works had the largest of the Oxford brick pits. It was dug to a depth of forty feet and worked until the beginning of the twentieth century when Morris Radiators was built over it.

The Randolph Street premises of Organ Brothers, the contractors, around 1900.

Starlings used to be one of Oxford's well-known traders. Their pill board men walked about St Ebbes and the town centre during a sale.

Some of the products of Axtell Perry Symm Masonry on Osney Mead, Oxford's recently developed Industrial Estate.

As well as its trades and industries Oxford has a strong marketing tradition. Gloucester Green was a thriving cattle market in 1895.

The cattle market moved to Oxpens, but was finally closed on 21 March 1979 to make way for an extension to the College of Further Education. The auctioneer shouts the bids at the last cattle market.

Oxford's Covered Market at Christmas 1909. Butcher Francis Terence Norton is wearing a white apron at Mr Kinch's butchers shop in the First Avenue.

The south end of Avenue 1 of the Covered Market in November 1936.

Palm's Delicatessen at the heart of the Covered Market on 8 December 1959.

Farming within the city limits used to occur on a surprising scale. Shepherd Wing with his dog and sheep off Horspath Road. He was an employee of the White family and lived in a cottage in Temple Road.

Haymaking on White's farm off Hollow Way on fields now occupied by council houses. Building the rick was a labour intensive process in 1901.

Gathering the hay on to the wagons at Hockmore Farm, Cowley, around 1915. Mr J. Willmott, the farmer, is on top of the left-hand cart.

Headington Hill Hall had a dairy business during the Morrell's time there. The Jersey cows were tended by milkmaids who also kept the inside of the dairy immaculate.

The widening of Magdalen Bridge in 1883 necessitated major engineering, as the scaffold platform and wheeled crane show.

Gloucester Green Fair was rather cramped. The side shows were squeezed up against the cattle pens.

St Clement's Fair took over the street between Rectory Road and the Plain.

St Giles Fair closes the street to traffic for two days in early September each year. It has always attracted large numbers of townspeople and the year 1907 was no exception.

A customer enjoys Mrs Bird's Gallopers at St Giles Fair in the 1920s.

The Oxford or Super Cinema in Magdalen Street in 1934. The cinema is now owned by the Cannon Group.

The Electra Cinema with the usherettes, box office and projection staff standing outside around 1910.

The choristers sing 'In the Merry Month of May' and the enormous crowd around Magdalen Bridge strains to hear. The custom takes place at 6.00 a.m. every May morning in Oxford. This one was in 1908.

A Morris Man as 'Hobby Horse' in front of the Radcliffe Camera on May Morning in 1983.

The Headington Quarry Morris Dancers at the Six Bells Public House on Whit Monday in 1914. William Kimber has the squeeze box, Number 1. is Teddy Hooper; 2. Todge Smith; 3. Harry 'Murderer' Green; 4. Unknown; 5. Shingle Smith; 6. Bill Kimber; 7. Hooper and 8. Sam Smith.

In Iffley on May morning in the 1900s the children have painstakingly dressed their garlands of flowers and leaves, to accompany their singing of May songs and help bring in the May money.

The savoury delights of a Headington Quarry Sheep Roast in 1900.

Oxford's medieval city walls run through New College gardens. They are still popular for a weekend stroll.

It appears that garden gnomes have been popular for a long time. These cheery chaps were found in Iffley Priory garden in 1912.

This courtyard of curiosities has been replaced by the Westgate Centre. In June 1901 the house stood off Church Street, St Ebbes.

Bins, bicycles and basins festoon the houses in Wyatt's Yard off St Aldates. It looked neat and tidy in the 1930s.

Children gather on a doorstep in Frederick Place on the south side of Castle Street in 1913.

This picturesque scene has now vanished forever. Castle Place shown here in 1913 was on the south side of Castle Street.

This photograph records Castle Place just before it was demolished in the 1930s.

A peg bag hangs ready in Pipemaker's Yard off St Aldates. None of the residents in the 1930s were pipe makers.

Potted plants brighten up the small alley called Franklin's Row on the south side of Castle Street, seen here in late August 1913.

These houses in Waterloo Buildings were just east of the old Trinity Street, St Ebbes. They themselves were built on the site of the priory of the Dominican Friars, Blackfriars.

A baby put to sleep outside Victoria Place off Queen Street.

A much less romantic view of a yard off St Aldates. This is Carters Yard in the 1930s with Joan Webb the tall girl on the left.

Albert Place off Castle Street in July 1914. Sawing logs was an all-year-round job before the days of gas and electric cookers.

There are still hidden places in Oxford. This is the view through the archway to 90–91 St Aldates in 1981. Was the little dog barking at the photographer?

Another hideaway in St Aldates. Number 89a looked like this in 1981.

In Barracks Lane stand the ruins of Bullingdon Castle, a sham, pictured in July 1914.

Frewin Court is surrounded by Oxford's busy central streets, but it is still attractive.

The lane from St Aldates Churchyard was a green and attractive place in 1890.

The narrow street of Clarks Row off St Aldates on 1 August 1904.

A woman pushes a pram through Friars Entry just before the First World War. The Gloucester Arms pub and Underhills can be seen on the left.

If you meet someone in Bulwarks Lane you have to stop and chat. The alley links George Street with New Road winding round Nuffield College.

Plough Yard, another residential side-street off St Aldates.

All the windows of these houses in Littlemore Court off St Aldates stay open in the summer warmth. For once they are not obscured by washing.

The city's own coat of arms. The red ox stands proudly on three waves of blue.

ACKNOWLEDGEMENTS

Oxfordshire Museums Service • Oxfordshire County Libraries • Oxford and County Newspapers • Curators of the Bodleian Library (Minn Collection 5/48A, 3/14, 5/35, 5/44, 6/55, 5/16, 1/19, 5/37, 6/16, 2/39, 5/27A, 5/27B, 5/29, 8/56, 7/23, 33/25, 8/71A, 3/13B, 5/15, 14/7B, 14/7, 5/35, 3/32, 2/19) • National Monuments Record • Oxford City Council • Austin-Rover Group Mr J. Evans • Mrs A. Hilsdon • Mr A. Taylor • Mr H. Mitchell Canon A.G. Whye • Mr L.J. Hawes • Mr Tyler • Miss Crisp • Mr Peacock Miss Norton • Mrs Marcham • Mr D. Gibbon • Mr J. Lardner-Coles.

Wherever possible the original donor or lender of a photograph has been acknowledged. I should like to thank all of them. In particular I should like to thank the staff of the local History Library in Oxford for their patience and interest, and Sue Etchells for typing the script. Above all I am grateful to Henry Taunt, photographer, whose skill and artistry made the compilation of this book a constant pleasure.